IMAGES
of England

STOURPORT-ON-SEVERN

A detail from James Sherriff's Perspective View of Stour Port, 1776. The canal company's great commercial hotel, later called the Tontine, was occupied by 1773. The gentry flocked in their carriages to see the wonders of the 'Bason' and the new bridge, and fashionable water parties were held before growing trade took over.

IMAGES
of England

STOURPORT-ON-SEVERN

Anna Carter
for Stourport Civic Society

TEMPUS

First published 2000
Reprinted 2004

Tempus Publishing Limited
The Mill, Brimscombe Port,
Stroud, Gloucestershire, GL5 2QG
www.tempus-publishing.com

British Library Cataloguing in Publication Data.
A catalogue record for this book is available from the British Library.

ISBN 0 7524 2058 5

Typesetting and origination by Tempus Publishing Limited.
Printed in Great Britain.

The *Lady Honor* pleasure steamer, moored near the barge lock below the Tontine and Severn
Side. Capt. Hatton of the Angel Hotel had the *Lady Honor* and the *May Queen* and daily ran
'pleasant river trips' to Holt Fleet in the holiday season. The *Lady Honor* could take 183
passengers.

Contents

Foreword

My memories of Stourport in the early part of the twentieth century are of a busy little town, with many factories which provided work for a population of around 4,000. The factories were Baldwins Rolling Mills, Wilden; Textile Carpets; Anglo Enamelware Ltd; Bond Worth Carpets; Gas Works; Holbrooks Vinegar Works; Baldwin Son & Co Ltd, Ironfounders; Thomas Vale & Sons Ltd, Builders; Beakbane Tannery. Those remaining in business today are Bond Worth and Thomas Vale & Sons Ltd.

The shops in Stourport, although relatively small, were varied enough to meet the demands, so it was not necessary for any shopper to go outside the town, whatever their needs. The shops that are still in business are Blunts Shoes, Bickerton hairdressers and Stanley Barten, tailors.

Stourport has always been a very popular town with Birmingham and Black Country people to visit for 'a day out', and at Bank Holidays crowds would be strolling from the railway station down to the river. Today the town still has its appeal, but now our visitors come by coach and car, whereas in those early days they came by excursion train.

In the early twentieth century the River Severn and the canal were used extensively for carrying commercial goods and today both are still busy waterways, but the traffic is for leisure and the 'good life'.

I appreciate very much being invited to write this foreword.

Fred Bevan

Mr Bevan was born in 1904. He started work in the time office at Anglo Enamelware Ltd at the age of thirteen, and from 1918-1924 was employed in the offices of the foundry. He joined Stourport's celebrated Town Band in 1922. The photograph shows Mr Bevan in 1993, pointing out the position of the boundary stone between Upper and Lower Mitton.

Introduction
Before the Canal

Lower Mitton was a chapelry of the parish of Kidderminster. The name Mitton is thought to come from the Anglo-Saxon word mythe, 'meeting of rivers or confluence'. In the Domesday Book of 1086, Mitton is listed as one of sixteen outliers held under Kidderminster by King William. It would appear that in 1086 there were three mills in the Manor of Kidderminster; one of these was in Lower Mitton.

The convent of Maiden Bradley in Wiltshire, who held the mill of Mitton for over 300 years, probably founded the chapel of St Michael at Mitton in the early thirteenth century. In 1625 the chapel and chapel yard was consecrated; a plaque in the church commemorates this occasion. Before this, the bodies of the people of Lower Mitton were taken to St Mary's church, Kidderminster, for burial. An inventory or terrier taken by George Dance in 1635 of the glebe lands belonging to the vicarage, refers to the 'chappell at a towneshipp called Nether Mitton in the sayd parish wch doth belong to the sayd Parish Church of Kidr' and includes the 'Chappell Church Yard containing one acre.' Other glebe land was in Chapell Hill, Church Field, Newland Gate, Wall Field, Old Follow, Priests Meadow, the Leigh, and Lampytt Field.

This original chapel was replaced in 1792 by a new church because it was 'a very ancient structure and greatly decayed in the foundation walls and roof, and notwithstanding the inhabitants have from time to time laid out several considerable sums of money in repairing it, yet the same by length of time is become so very ruinous and decayed in every part that it cannot any longer be supported but must be wholly taken down and rebuilt.' The church has subsequently been replaced twice. The surviving parish registers start in 1693, but the Bishops' Transcripts take the records of baptisms, marriages and burials back to 1603, apart from a gap during the Civil War.

In the sixteenth century the manor was held by the Lygon family. In the seventeenth century it passed to the Clents and then to the Folliotts. It was sold to John Craven from Yorkshire in the early 1800s. Lower Mitton's main occupation was agriculture. Before the seventeenth century there is evidence that the agricultural economy was based on an open field system. The main fields were Lye, Long, Owld Fallowe, Lampitt, Wall Field, Church Field, and Sloe Hill. Small fields were called the Closse, Mythe, Moore, Short Lands, Great Woodcroft and Little Woodcroft. Those fields lying along the rivers, Lye, Long, Lampitt and Mythe, were used as meadows, while those more inland were arable fields. Later, the fields were divided up into individual holdings. Inventories show evidence of a rural economy with references to a bull, oxen, horses, cattle, a number of pigs, and a large number of sheep. Bees and poultry were also kept. Corn, hay, rye and barley were cultivated, along with some hemp, flax, hops, wheat and apples. There are occasional references to fishing nets and boats. Inside the houses were beef, bacon and cheese as well as wool, linen and flax yarn. Old wills show the major occupation as yeoman, but some men described themselves as husbandman. Other occupations include fisher(man), carpenter, wheelwright, blacksmith, collar maker, sythesmith, forgeman, tailor and weaver. Two members of the clergy also left wills. The majority of the people lived in the area around what is now Gilgal and Mitton Street. Other families lived near Long Lane – the road to Lickhill, and the road to Kidderminster. The population in 1676, according to the Churchwardens' Presentments, was 98.

John Leland in his descriptions of his travels through England around 1535 says, 'From Bewdley to Mitton village about a 4 miles by woody ground and some corne in enclosures. Here dothe Stoure ryver breke into 2 or 3 armelets, and servythe mills.' As well as the fulling mills belonging to the Willmott family in the seventeenth century, there was also the presence of the iron industry in Mitton. A list of forges in England and Wales, produced in 1750, shows Jenny Hole Forge producing 450 tons of bar iron per year and Mitton Lower Forge producing 400 tons per year. The Lower Forge produced wrought iron from bar or pig iron imported from other areas in Britain for the nail industry of the West Midlands, and the forge was also used for tinning the sheet iron or blackplate produced at Bringewood Ironworks, Shropshire. Although these forges are described as Mitton forges, they were actually situated in Hartlebury Parish.

So Lower Mitton was essentially a rural village with a small, but growing population until the middle of the eighteenth century. Since the Romans left Britain, the roads were always in a terrible condition, which made the transportation of both raw materials and finished goods very difficult. Water transport had always been used to move goods and materials. But there were problems using the rivers due to droughts, floods and other difficulties. Early attempts to improve the rivers had not been very successful. The Duke of Bridgewater employed James Brindley to build a canal to carry his coals cheaply to Manchester. It was finished in 1761 and cut the cost of coal by half, showing that this was the way forward. If the four major rivers in England – the Mersey, Severn, Thames and Trent – could be linked by canals, the breakages would be reduced, as would the costs of raw materials. The first development in this scheme was the Trent and Mersey Canal. The next stage was to connect this canal with the River Severn; this was to be the Staffordshire and Worcestershire Canal.

The inhabitants of Bewdley were supporters of the bill, submitting a petition from 'The Bailiff, Burgesses, Justices, Aldermen, Merchants, Clergy and Tradesmen of this Borough of Bewdley in the County of Worcester whose names are hereunto subscribed' to Parliament for an Act to be passed. When the Act of Parliament was passed in 1766, it stated that its southern terminal was to be 'at some place between Bewdley and Titton Brook.' The line of the canal was surveyed by Hugh Henshall and Samuel Simcock. James Brindley was the chief engineer, but because he was busy with other projects, the canal was constructed by Thomas Dadford and his sons, with the help of the Clerk of Works, John Baker. It was evident that if the canal were to terminate at Bewdley, a tunnel would have to be constructed under the hill between Kidderminster and Bewdley, which would be very expensive in terms of time and money. It would be much easier to build the canal along the valley of the River Stour and so the canal came to Lower Mitton, in use from the Severn to Wolverhampton in 1771, and completed the following year.

From an article on Lower Mitton by Francesca Llewellyn, former Stourport Librarian

Note on the 2004 Reprint

Inevitably there have been some changes in Stourport since this book was first published in 2000: Fred Bevan died shortly after the book's publication and Anna Carter died the following year, in 2001. The Tontine Hotel (p.2) now stands empty, awaiting restoration; the Bond Worth carpet factory (p.75) has ceased production and the site is to be redeveloped; the Drill Hall (p.94) has been demolished but the Sergeant-Instructor's House has been retained as part of the residential development of the site; and the White Lion (p.67) has been converted into flats.

The area of Lower Mitton a century ago. The unfamiliar scene at the top is now Church Avenue. The Girls' School is on the corner, with a sign board to Lower Mitton church. Pictured below right and left are the main routes of the hamlet, now Mitton Street and Gilgal, with the River Stour in flood.

The riverside just below the Angel, probably in the 1920s. The wharf belonged to Peter Price, who sold land to the canal proprietors for their port development. The graving docks of the inner basin, the gasworks and the old cottages where the tug master lived make a group which spans the town's history.

Cottages on Severn Side, probably in the 1920s. The family group is on the steps of the former Cross Inn, which closed in the early 1880s. Until around 1710 it was used by the clothiers of Worcester, who brought their woollen cloth by barge to this quay, to be fulled in the mills of Hartlebury parish. It was known as the 'staking', 'stacking' or 'cloth house' and the ancient building on the left was originally the warehouse.

The lane to Walshe's Farm, off 'The Rough', around 1904. These old cottages, which were in the parish of Lower Areley, faced onto the route to the Redstone crossing. The ferry was discontinued when the bridge was built for the new canal port in 1775.

One
Basins and Canal

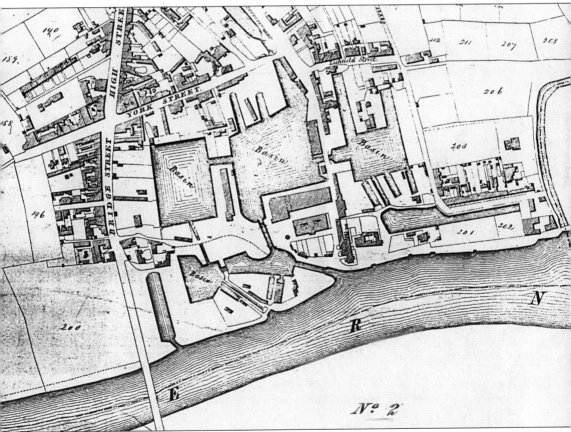

From the 'Plan of the Chapelrey of Lower Mitton', 1849. It shows the port complex at its maximum extent. Remains, believed to be the end of the basin along Cheapside, were found during work at the vinegar brewery many years ago.

View from the top floor of York House, possibly in the 1920s. This photograph scanned from a tiny print, conveys the impressive expanse of the upper basins and warehouses, and shows boats moored alongside the cranes on the wharf. Elm trees in those days were part of the Worcestershire landscape.

Trows in the old basin around the end of the nineteenth century. This basin and the barge locks were the first phase of the canal port, expanded ten years later in 1781 by another upper basin and narrow beam locks to the river. Masts swaying above the warehouses, as in James Sherriff's engraving, must have been an impressive sight. The turret clock was made by Samuel Thorp of Abberley in 1813, paid for by public subscription. The Canal Company gave seven guineas and offered the site on their warehouse 'till a better situation could be found'.

DANKS, VENN & CO.

'Having taken up the Business lately carried on by

BELSHAM & Co.

RESPECTFULLY INFORM THEIR FRIENDS THAT THEIR

LOCK-UP TROWS,

REGULARLY SAIL TWICE A WEEK,

TO AND FROM

Bristol, Glo'ster, Worcester, Stourport & Bewdley;

And by their own Boats to Stourbridge, &c.

By which every description of GOODS, particularly Wines and Spirits, are safely and expeditiously conveyed for the undermentioned Places;

LUDLOW	WOLVERHAMPTON	BIRMINGHAM	MANCHESTER	AND ALL PARTS
SHREWSBURY	THE STAFFORDSHIRE	COVENTRY	AND ALL PARTS	OF THE WEST
KIDDERMINSTER	IRON WORKS AND	LEICESTER	OF THE NORTH	SWANSEA
STOURBRIDGE	POTTERIES	DERBY	BATH	AND
DUDLEY	WALSALL	LIVERPOOL	EXETER	SOUTH WALES

FOR PARTICULARS OF FREIGHT, &C., APPLY TO

WM. BIRD, Wharfinger, } *Stourport;*
DANKS, VENN & CO.
JOHN DANKS, Wharf, *Birmingham;*
CROWLEY & CO. *Wolverhampton;*
HOOD & WALL, Diglis, *Worcester;*

ANTWIS & STURLAND, Castle Fields, *Manchester,* or Duke's Dock, *Liverpool;*
W. KENDALL, Wharfinger, *Gloucester;*
T. Y. VENN, Wharfinger, 6, Tontine Warehouse, Quay Head, *Bristol.*

D. V. & Co. request the favor of their Friends to be particular in directing Goods UPON THE PACKAGES to be forwarded by their Trows. [MARY NICHOLSON, PRINTER, BRIDGE-STREET, STOURPORT.]

A notice for Danks, Venn & Co, Carriers, dating from around 1830-1835. It was printed by Mary Nicholson, who continued the business after the death of her husband, the eminent printer George Nicholson, in 1825 (see p. 118).

A wooden cantilever crane on a card posted in 1904. The crane's post is broken and it may have been in service since the basin was built. There is an engraving of 1814 showing a similar crane on the canal at Kidderminster. Boatmen probably used the garden door from the wharf opposite, to go for their meals in the basement of York House. The terrace of York House bears the date 1787. Visible on York Street is the sign of the Wellington Vaults.

Boat-building near the lower barge lock around 1910. The dry dock had an unusual drawbridge gate. In the days of steam tugs, coal was wheeled through a tunnel from the building on the left to the river quay. One wall of pierced brickwork is all that remains of the various workshops of this lower area known as 'the island'.

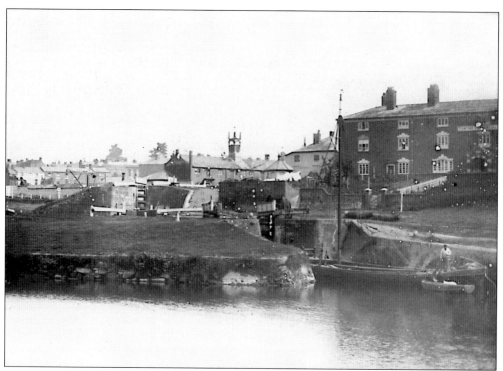

A trow at the entrance to the barge lock, possibly in the 1880s.

A day boat which had delivered slack for the power station, 1948. The warehouse along the south side of the basin was still there when Eric de Maré took his memorable photographs of canal architecture in Stourport and wrote 'The Canals of England'.

A few years later, in the early fifties, another fine photographer was recording the canal landscape: Ashley Moulden, an Australian who came to Stourport in 1952 and stayed to work with the Abbotts, building canal cruisers. His photographs (see pp. 20, 30, 31 and 69) and those of de Maré record the grandeur and decay of the basins and surroundings, taken before the sweeping demolitions of the later 1950s. Curved walls, archways, ramps – to quote Tony Conder of the National Waterways Museum, it was 'the engineer building for his motive power, the horse'. Black and white photography has unforgettably conveyed these functional structures worn by time.

Arthur Phillips outside his house, No. 9 Tontine Buildings, probably in the late 1930s. Behind him is the warehouse demolished around 1950. The houses along the west wing of the Tontine have been empty since the last resident moved out in 1972. A major public inquiry was held in 1977, at which canal and conservation organizations successfully defended the Tontine against plans to partially demolish it.

A family group in front of the 'round house', the octagonal toll office, late 1920s. From left to right: Phoebe Cook, her daughter Amy, Florrie Powell, William Powell and Albert Cook. Beyond the car is No. 8 Tontine Buildings. There is further reference to the toll office on p. 37.

The tarpaulin workshop of the Severn and Canal Carrying Company in the 1930s. The unidentified worker is posing with his materials for making top cloths for workboats. The sail loft was over the arched passageway at the top of Severn Side.

Holbrook's vinegar brewery boat, *Sabrina*, in the bottom locks, date unknown. From left to right: Jimmy Bourne who was responsible for the boat, Charlie Vaughan, Reg Abbotts, Den Newey, Bill Millichip and Jimmy Wood. The boat was registered in 1912 or 1913 and took casks through to Holbrooks, Ashted Row, Birmingham. Across the basin is the Beam Engine House, which until 1914 still had its Boulton and Watt steam engine, ordered in 1804.

Skating on the basin in the winter of 1952. The skaters, Holt and Florence Abbott with their daughter Julia, were living on their boat, *Rothesay*, while building and hiring canal cruisers from their workshop on the wharf. In 1958 they exchanged premises with British Waterways and moved to the former maintenance yard on the canal. Holt was one of the tireless campaigners who saw a future for inland waterways at a time when talk amongst councillors was of health hazards and of making the basin into a car park.

British Waterways' workshop on the basin in 1990, the first premises of Canal Pleasurecraft (Stourport).

The launching of Tavy Cleave in 1957. The Abbotts had a slip-way made on the basin. Standing by the flag is Holt's sister, Betty Abbott, who painted canal ware in the canal office by York Street lock.

British Waterways' hire boat, *Water Vole*, around 1960. *Water Vole*, like *Water Vixen*, was a work boat which was cut down and converted as a hire boat in the late 1950s. At that time British Waterways produced a series of cruising booklets designed to meet the growing interest in the canals for holidays. Second from the left, near the 1958 Jaguar, is Horace Redding, who helped to organize fund-raising to renovate the clock warehouse for Stourport Yacht Club.

Warehouses and houses on Mart Lane in the early to mid fifties. The LMS depot on the left handled vinegar brought from Holbrooks by dray, Worths carpets and other goods. It had a stable at the far end. The vast warehouse known as the 'long room' (see p. 2) had a small house at its northern end. Beyond that is Bond Worth's chimney, the last of Stourport's industrial stacks, which were a feature of the skyline for much of the late nineteenth and twentieth centuries.

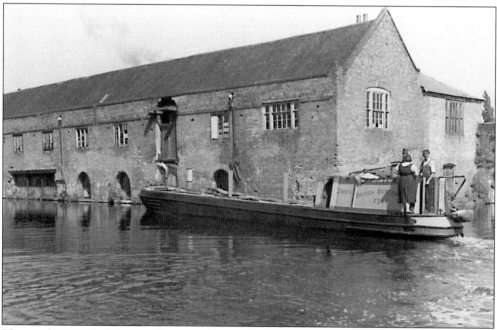

The southern end of the warehouse and New Basin Bridge, No. 3. A British Waterways work boat, the *Gambia*, is going through to the Mart Lane basin. *Gambia* was built in 1907 for the Fellows, Morton & Clayton fleet. The steep unmade 'bank' and bridge were at one time popularly named after a trow master, Capt. Dark, of Mart Lane. The building next to the bridge was the office of the Severn & Canal Carrying Company.

The lock house by the top barge lock, in the 1920s or earlier. It was known as No. 11 Tontine Buildings at one time. It was the home of Phyl and Phil Garrett, who was lock keeper for twenty years from 1974, following John Modley.

Phil Garrett, lock-keeper, in his office in 1976. Phil had worked on the canals and was for many years captain of his own pair of boats, carrying goods between London Limehouse Dock, Manchester Docks and the Midlands. He built up a store of knowledge about Stourport Basins and their past, which he willingly shared.

The clock warehouse, 1960. Stourport Yacht Club, founded in 1949, had taken on the building in 1958 and were in the process of repairing it. The Georgian warehouse on the right was demolished in 1996 to make way for development. At one time it was used by Cotterells, who had a boat raft on the river. It later became George Head's machine shop and timber store.

Dismantling an old boat raft, date unknown. The warehouse had its own sluice or arm for unloading, which was filled in when the warehouse was pulled down. The raft was an old Dutch barge which had been cut down and converted for hiring out punts. The old police station can be seen across York Street.

The original canal bridge on York Street, Wallfield Bridge No. 4. It was rebuilt in 1938, without the viewing hole in the high parapet wall. On the right are buildings facing Lichfield Street (see p. 24).

The new bridge almost completed. This series of photographs on pp. 23 and 24 were taken by Thomas Cox, whose father was a tug master and had worked on the trows out of Gloucester.

The buildings being demolished at the top of Mart Lane. The occupants of the small house on the rounded corner could fish out of their back window. The warehouse was built over the water and boats went underneath to unload.

Demolition of the old Wallfield Bridge. In the background are Bell Row, Mr Large's hardware shop and the two terraced houses rebuilt as three around 1959. York Street Lock was once known as Cotton's Lock.

A view across the inner basin and Bond Worth factory to the Worcester Road in 1933. In the early 1800s, various plans were put forward for extending the canal port. The inner basin, the scheme chosen, was built between 1806-1810 and had an entrance up onto the wharves from Lichfield Street. This 'New Basin' vastly increased the reservoir capacity of the upper basins. On the south side there were boatbuilding and repair yards, with three dry docks and a wide-beam lock to a further basin (see p. 11), which was constructed in 1810-1812. Before the river basin and new engine house were built around 1805, there was an old engine house, aqueduct and covered feeder which conveyed water from the Stour, to raise the level of the old basin when it became too low. The carpet factory developed round this core of old industrial buildings on the Stour. Nearby, upstream, was the ancient mill and carpet manufacturing area of Farm Bed (between Baldwin Road and the Worcester Road.) The slack boats along the coal wharf on the east side of the inner basin were unloaded by travelling cranes and the coal carried in hoppers on a conveyor over Severn Road. From there it went by rail to the power station, which had started operating in 1926. The Lombardy poplars along the coal wharf were planted by Bullocks Nursery around this time. Up the hill beyond the basin, behind Bell Row and the immaculate garden strips, there is the line of south-facing Georgian cottages of Lion Yard and the stables of the Lion Hotel. Before Stourport sprang up with the coming of the canal, there were old routes crossing the area, which were recorded on a colour-coded plan by James Sherriff in 1802. Mitton Street was on the Long Lane from Lickhill to Hartlebury. There was a toll-gate on the road to Worcester. Severn Road, earlier known as Severn Lane and before that Price's Lane, led to the river wharf; and a route along Lichfield Street and past Lichfield House crossed the fields to the Stour. Lichfield House, now offices of Carpets of Worth, was in the latter 1800s the family residence of Thomas Bond Worth, founder of the Company.

The inner basin and Severn Lane around the 1880s. Though so damaged, it is worth including this rare record of the working basin. A trow with a striped sail lies near the dock building, with the Tontine and Severn Side beyond. Much ballast must have been needed for trows to pass through the bridge hole to the main basin.

The coal wharf of the Shropshire, Worcestershire & Staffordshire Electric Power Company and the conveyor across Severn Road.

A corner of the docks, Cheapside and the gasworks, possibly in the 1930s. The dock of Bakers, boat and barge builders, was in this corner of the inner basin around the turn of the twentieth century. The Stourport Gas, Coal & Coke Co Ltd, 1865, built their works on part of the short-lived 1812 basin, extending over the whole site in 1878. Tube Plastics (TP Activity Toys) purchased the disused gasworks in 1961, moving to Stourport from Cradley Heath. The Royal Oak is just visible behind the poplars.

Gateway to the docks from Severn Road, photographed in 1989, with Mrs Margaret Downton.

Swans nesting in a sunken boat near Lichfield Street, 1950s. Corbetts crane and stacked wood are near the old entrance to the basin, where drays brought the timber up into the woodyard.

The inner basin in its last days, silted up and partly infilled, late 1950s. Permission was given in 1960 to fill the basin, and the bridge on Mart Lane was demolished. The Canal Company's blacksmith, Charlie Perkins, used to live in one of the wharf cottages on the left, inside the old gateway. At the top of Lichfield Street was Bowens Bakery and on the corner, Mrs Jones's sweetshop; over it was once said to have been the flare loft, used in regulating the basin level. By the date of this aerial view, the great warehouse on Mart Lane had gone.

Some of the Griffiths family with Hetty Bullock at No. 4 Mart Lane in 1947. The Waterways cottages in Mart Lane and Severn Side, like the Tontine Buildings, tended to house a settled community, sometimes passing from one generation to the next. One neighbour of the Griffiths was Mr Moverley, a skilled violin-maker.

A windy day on the upper basin, 1989. The covered wet dock on the right was used for the *Lady Hatherton*, the Company Committee boat, whose centenary was celebrated in 1998. The Georgian 'New Warehouse,' with its dock arm alongside, stands imposingly in the centre (see p. 22).

The remarkable footbridge which linked the Canal Company's yard with their property across the canal. This is also a rare undated record of the original Lower Mitton Bridge No. 5 rebuilt in 1928. The famous Tannery stack was reduced in height in 1910.

Gambia (see p. 20) moored on the canal below Lion Hill, early 1950s. Boat horses used to go up to the stables in Lion Yard behind the hotel (see p. 67). The Underhills' little house was demolished in the fifties. In the early 1900s, T.H. Hoult, ale merchants, bottled Guinness in the canal-side building for sale at No. 4 High Street; and Hoult & Landon were auctioneers.

Gambia at British Waterways main depot on the canal, early 1950s. The tin-clad shed in the yard was a feature of the canal, dismantled in 1991. The lock gates for the whole of the Staffordshire and Worcestershire Canal used to be made there; the machinery worked by a steam boiler. Trees from Corbetts' yard were floated up through the lock.

The crane at the yard. The moored cruiser, *Kingfisher*, was built by Canal Pleasurecraft for a private owner.

Canal Pleasurecraft in 1979, when the business was sold to Dartline.

Two
River Severn

Cotterells landing stage above Stourport Bridge, from a postcard sent in 1914. It shows Mrs Cotterell, Minnie and Reg, and Clem Hamblin. Next along was Buckleys landing stage and then the 'floating swimming bath'. A trip to Stourport offered, 'the tranquil surroundings and recuperative air of the river-side, the fields and the woods.'

The first Stourport bridge, from a drawing by Samuel Ireland.

A possibly unique photograph of the second bridge.

The stone bridge, whose foundations still remain in the riverbed, was opened in 1775 and became at once a fashionable attraction. On the 'compleatest' occasion a party came down the river from Ticknell House, 'with French Horns and other Music ... and as their Coming was expected they were saluted with guns as they passed and re-passed the New Bridge.' (Berrows 1775).

The second bridge was built in 1806, some years after the stone bridge was damaged by floods. It was 'most extraordinary and remarkable', a single iron arch, 'of 150 feet span, and about 50 feet perpendicular above the water.' (W. Pitt, 1810). *The Cambrian Traveller's Guide* said the bridge was cast by founders in the neighbourhood. There is an engraving of the second bridge by Thomas Wheeldon, a copper-plate printer of Stourport. It is also one of the views by J.P. Neale in the *Beauties of England and Wales*, published in 1815.

Sixty years later, traffic demanded a wider bridge and the second bridge was dismantled. Isaac Wedley (see p. 122) recalled the seemingly-precarious wooden bridge which was built as the temporary crossing until the new bridge was opened in 1870. The present handsome structure has featured in a host of postcard views all through the twentieth century.

The floating bandstand above the bridge, early 1900s. The cottages seen beyond the crowd are in Court 2, Bridge Street, and were demolished around 1935. Mr C. Cotterell built the bandstand and Stourport Town Band kept it in the river basin in front of the Crown. They gave it an annual coat of tar fetched from the gasworks.

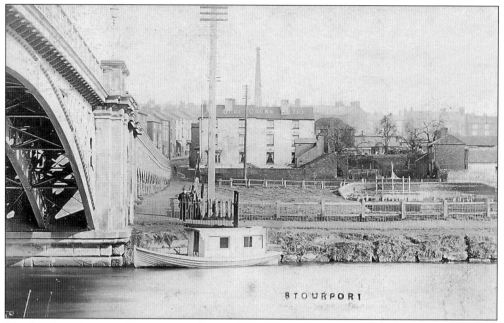

The bandstand moored in the river basin, 1906. The Olde Crown Hotel was rebuilt in the 1930s and the little row of cottages on Engine Lane was demolished when the Crown was extended. The original brickwork of the flood arches is on the east side seen here. The west side was extended for the extra width of the new bridge of 1870.

Enjoying the frozen river in a big freeze of the late 1800s. There were periods of exceptionally deep cold in 1874, 1878-1879, 1881, 1890 and 1895.

Looking downstream from the bridge, before the First World War. The old swing-bridge crosses the basin entrance, and by the Riverside Café is one of Capt. Sam Palmer's saloon steamers, the *Amo*, which took passengers to Holt Fleet daily and parties as far as Tewkesbury and Gloucester. Capt. Palmer lived at No. 11 Bridge Street, now the Severn Tandoori Restaurant.

One of the great floods of the 1940s. The octagonal toll office by the Tontine was similar to those at the Bratch and Stewponey, a design that belongs to the Staffs & Worcs Canal (see p. 16). It was demolished in the early 1950s.

The steam tug *Athlete* pulling a train of sailing trows, taken from a photograph/postcard posted in Stourport in 1911.

Bond Worth weavers, brought out to sweep the ice for skating, probably the same date as the scene on p. 36. They are on the river near the entrance to the barge locks.

A busy scene on the river in the early 1900s. Beyond Captain Hatton's steamer are the trow *Usk* and the tug *Pioneer*. The Boat Club-house opposite was built in 1901. Sometimes there were twenty canal boats waiting to catch the Worcester tug, six o'clock prompt every morning.

The tug *Pioneer* and the *Lady Honor*.

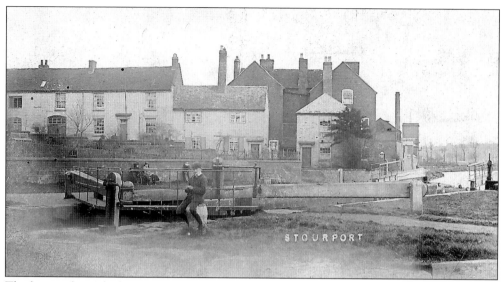

The bottom barge lock and the stables and cottages of Severn Side. Beyond the gasworks and vinegar brewery is the view of open landscape before the power station was built.

A trow at the wharf in front of the Angel about 1900, when it was kept by Bessie Beaman. The notice over the side door advertises stabling. Behind are the workshops on the docks. The terrace on the left was demolished in the late 1950s.

Jack Knight at No. 11 Severn Side, with salmon he had caught at the Hampstall, 1950s. Caught with rod and line in late March time, the largest, the hen, was about thirty pounds. Some of the catch would go to Simpsons the salmon factors in Kidderminster, later MacFisheries.

The handsome frontage of buildings on Severn Side in the early 1900s. There was a grocer's shop kept by the Barber family at No. 5 Severn Side, on the corner with the Venetian window.

Ernest Knight and the industrial scene below the Angel, dominated by the gasworks' retort house. Opposite there were lapwings wheeling over the river meadows. Behind Mr Knight is the *Severn Collier*, the last boat to be built in the old yard on the inner basin.

The countryside south of the river, around 1930. *Mervic*, a converted submarine chaser ML319 belonging to Vic Webb, is moored on the right. The houseboats are the *Joyce*, the *Daisy* and *Lorraine*.

Cottages by the former Cross Inn around 1906 (see p. 10). The children are Leonora and Lily Shellis. An empty 'Severner' is approaching and the tow path looks well used. The Scots pines in the distance mark the former hermitage and crossing at Redstone.

A house on the path at the top of Redstone cliff, before the First World War. At one time ramblers could get refreshments there. Below the caves, near the crossing, was a three-storey house, divided into two cottages and bearing the date 1685. It was demolished in the mid-1930s.

'The Eel Catcher, 1864, by Benjamin Williams Leader RA.' The painter, born in 1831, was the son of the great civil engineer, Edward Leader Williams of Diglis House, Worcester, where John Constable was a frequent visitor. The eel catcher is sitting in his traditional Severn punt at Water Lug below Redstone.

Edward Leader Williams, inspecting the sunken boats at Lincombe in the 1850s. He designed the great locks and weirs which improved navigation from Gloucester to Stourport after the Parliamentary Act of 1842.

Lincombe Lock, early 1900s. There were two lock-keepers in the days when the paddles were operated manually. The beautiful cliff beyond was known as the Bay; the old course of the river was off on the left.

A pleasure steamer passing through Lincombe Lock on its way to Holt Fleet around 1914. The glazed porch on the lock-keeper's house gave him a view of the approaches in both directions. Lincombe was one of the most popular postcard scenes.

Trows moored in the Floating Harbour by Bristol Bridge around the 1880s. The quay near St Nicholas's church is known as the Welsh Back because 'The Float' was used by trows from the river ports. This treasured photograph came from the family of John Taylor of Severn Side, Stourport, who worked on the trows for many years. It was a rough and risky life and needed the finest seamanship; they sailed all round the Channel ports. Trows were towed through the shallows of the estuary using the power of the tide. Three men rowed the tow boat and they would nurse the trow in the lanes they knew. On one occasion a trow struck something, ripped the bottom out and sank before the crew could untie the tow-rope. They went down with the trow. Ever after, an axe was carried in the tow boat to cut the tow-rope through.

Three
Churches

The fine Jacobean and Georgian rectory at Areley Kings, early 1900s. George Nicholson's *Cambrian Traveller's Guide*, printed just over the river in 1813, calls the church and rectory upon a summit, 'a spot neatly embellished'. The 'out-stout', the garden house, was built by Richard Vernon in 1728. The Revd Daniel Vawdrey fitted it with shelves made from the sails of the windmill, which he converted into a house around 1900, (can be seen in the distance on p. 22).

General Booth at the Wesleyan church, 18 August 1904. William Booth, founder of the Salvation Army, was on an evangelical journey by motor car from Land's End to Aberdeen. When the five cars reached Stourport, 'the Union Jack floated from the top of the principal carpet factory' and the workers formed into line outside the gates, the women in their white aprons and blouses.

Lower Mitton church on the site of the old chapel. (see p. 7). Built in the Italian style, the church was approached from Church Avenue through ornamental gates. 'Church where we were married,' writes the sender of the postcard in 1926.

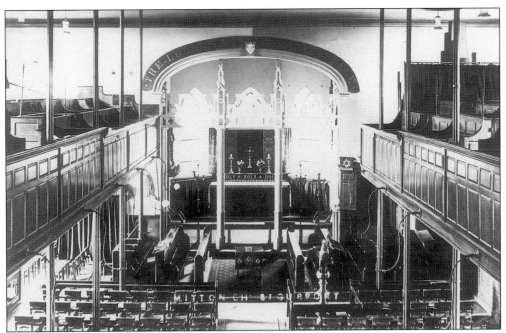
The interior of the Georgian Mitton church. It had gas lighting by 1855.

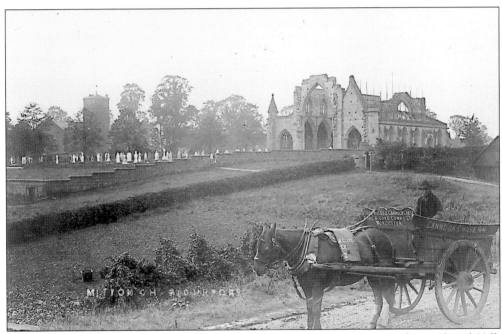
The new St Michael's church under construction near the Georgian church on Chapel Hill. Work began in 1882 and it was consecrated in 1910. Though the Revd Benjamin Gibbons's ambitious scheme was never completed, the town had a church of Victorian grandeur. It was demolished in 1979, after storm damage. The cart is from the South Wales & Cannock Chase Coal and Coke Company's yard at the station.

St Michael's church Sunday school around 1946. At the head of 'Oranges and Lemons' in the carnival parade are John and Roy Shimmin, Brian Bird, Jill Wainwright, Janet Hicks and Frankie Humphries. It started from the old parish rooms in Bewdley Road and was organized by Miss Freda Jones, whose pet food stall in the old Market Hall is well remembered.

The Gypsy Mission Tent on Hartlebury Common, 1904. It was organised by Wesley Baker and pitched at the top of the common, opposite the Mount. In 1914 a permanent chapel was built, and the bell from old Mitton church called the thriving congregation to prayer.

Four
Round the Town

Areley House and the skyline of Stourport, in the 1920s. Areley House, built around 1780 and mentioned in the *Cambrian Traveller's Guide* of 1813, was later in the nineteenth century the residence of Joseph Rogers. The chimney of the tannery, then owned by Joseph and his brother, John Crane Rogers of the Heath, can be seen in the distance. The house became a private hotel after the First World War.

Stourport Bridge in the 1920s. The errand boy with his bicycle is George Baylis, who worked for Pearks, the High Street grocers, and went on to become manager.

Bridge Street in 1901. On the left were Hodges & Sons, Carriers, who ran a regular service to Worcester and Kidderminster. The terminus of the Kidderminster & Stourport Electric Tramway, opened in 1898, was at the bottom of Bridge Street. Trams were allowed to travel at eight miles per hour through the town.

Pheysey Ltd, Ironmongers' and Builders' Merchants, around 1898. Third from right is George Gittins, apprentice wheelwright. His brother Sid was apprenticed to Fathers, blacksmiths. Pheyseys also had No. 24 Bridge Street, opposite, which was taken over by Buftons.

Bridge Street, late 1950s. By this date Burgess Motors had taken over Pheysey's former premises. On the corner of Raven Street, in the foreground, is No. 15 Bridge Street, which was George Nicholson's 'house and printing office' (see p. 118) in the early 1800s.

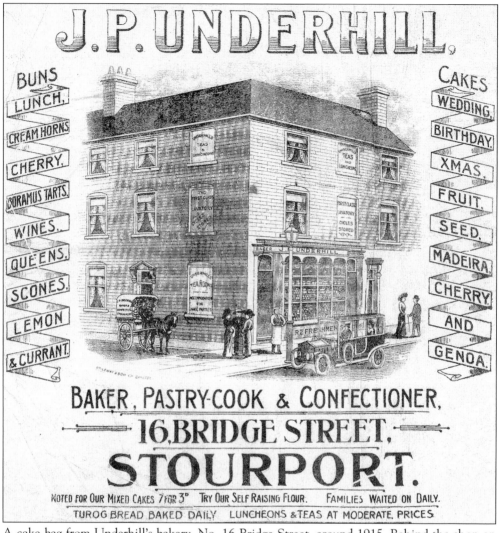

A cake bag from Underhill's bakery, No. 16 Bridge Street, around 1915. Behind the shop on the corner of Raven Street was the sitting room, bakehouse with flour loft over it, confectioners den, an assembly room over a large dining room, yard and stables. The delivery horses were turned out in a field at the end of Raven Street.

The 1956 carnival parade passing Buftons, Nos 23-24 Bridge Street. Pheysey's original ironmonger's shop was taken over by James Bufton in 1912 and continued in business for nearly seventy years. This was one of the finest shop fronts in the town. Tradition has it that the surgeons, Richard Jukes and Kenrick Watson, had their practice at No. 24 Bridge Street, though some evidence suggests they were in the High Street, (see p. 117).

The old Town Hall and Market Hall in 1963. In an elegant notice one hundred years earlier, the Stourport Reading Institution announced: 'Another Glimpse of the Western World', a lecture by John Slaney Packington, Esq., to be held at the Town Hall, front seats one shilling. The Town Hall was built in 1833 and demolished in 1973.

The High Street, probably around 1914-1918. On the left was the bank, where the 1964 post office now stands. Once known as the Mansion, it was said to have been built by Richard Jukes. In a succession of changes the Metropolitan Bank became the Midland Bank, and the present bank was built in the grounds of Bank House, which had a beautiful high-walled garden. (see pp. 95 and 117.)

The Wheatsheaf in the 1960s. The gift shop was formerly Jack Birch's cobblers shop, where he was still working in 1951 at the age of eighty-three. Behind the Piccolo Café there was a hall where Stourport Civic Society, formed in 1968, held some of its first meetings. The photograph was taken by Tom Baylis.

Grainger's Butchers shop, No. 42 High Street. On the right is the old post office. Martins Bank later converted Grainger's premises, now Barclays Bank.

The Barten family with visitors, outside No. 25 High Street, around 1954. The Australians were on a round-the-world trip in an old London taxi. Ted Barten is second from left, then Mary and Freda Barten, with Stanley in front.

Stanley Barten Outfitters, splendidly decorated for the Coronation of George VI, 1937. Stanley Barten, senior, came to Stourport from Kent where he had been apprenticed as an outfitter at Weekes department store in Tunbridge Wells. He came to work at the tailors and outfitters, Minton, on the corner of York Street and Bridge Street, around 1900. From there he took on G. Ward's former little tobacconist's shop at No. 24 High Street, and expanded the tobacconist business into outfitting. A photograph taken ten years later around 1916 shows Nos 24 and 25 as a double fronted shop, with bay windows above; the conversion was carried out by Millners. The shop later extended into No 23 High Street, which had been Glovers boot and shoe shop. The tobacconist side of the business continued until the retirement of Mrs Freda Barten in 1994.

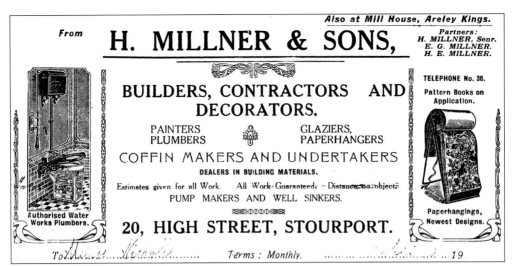

Millner's letterhead in 1919. There were some very fine examples of their sign writing for businesses in the town.

An outing setting off from Millner's in the late 1920s. Ernest Millner is standing in the doorway. The party is probably off to Aberystwyth. An earlier photograph exists showing Millner's workforce and these High Street premises before a shop front was installed. Here, half is still a residential frontage.

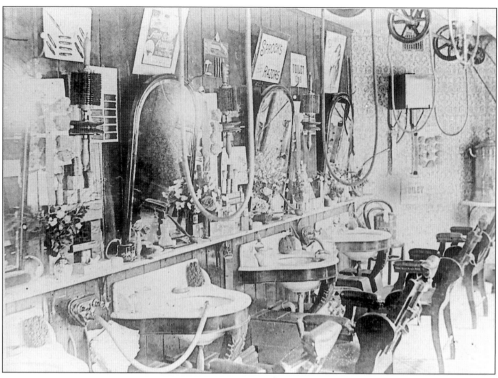

Bickertons Barbers shop, established in 1832. No. 19 High Street had previously been a school for girls. Seen here about 1900, the shop has its advanced system of machine brushes, probably the only one in the Midlands. The gleaming copper urn was still in place fifty years later. George Leslie Bickerton succeeded his father, Thomas, 'Tom', in 1940; Bill Bickerton started in the business in 1950.

A leaflet for Bickerton & Son, date uncertain. Thomas Price Bickerton, grandfather of Bill Bickerton, used to wind many local clocks including the tannery and the old post office clock, which was made by Bickertons; he also cycled out to Abberley and Astley Halls. In the days of George 'Les' Bickerton, his brother Bill, from W. Henn's in Wolverhampton, assisted with the clock repair side of the business.

A funeral at the Methodist church, probably in the early 1920s. T.B. Ketley's funeral cars from Coleman's Garage in Lombard Street are lined up in front of Haywoods Printing Office, E. Jones, Cobbler, and Jack Lashford's renowned Sweet & Ice-cream shop.

'Our New Bus.' The Allen Motor Omnibus Company started a service along the Stourport-Kidderminster tram route in 1913. Competition with trams was so intense that the normal three pence tram fare was cut to one penny. The Victoria Coffee Tavern at the top of the High Street became Roberts, The Chemist.

The Swan Hotel and top of the High Street, around 1907. The winged wheel sign showed that the Swan was recommended by the Cyclists Touring Club. There is a grocery on each corner: R. Evans, H. Riches (also wines and spirits) and W.H. Turner. The tramlines ran up Lombard Street, the main route through the town until Vale Road was built in 1923-1924.

Marsh & Baxter, No. 5 High Street, around 1938. Posing for the photograph are Jim Howells, manager, Geoff Pound, Margaret Bourne the cashier, and Bert Shinton.

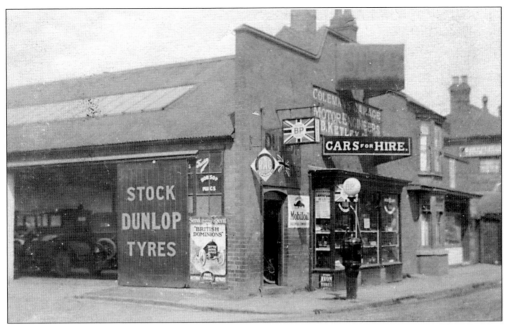

Coleman's Garage on the corner of Tan Lane and Lombard Street, in the mid to late 1920s. The proprietor was Thomas B. Ketley, who also owned the Station Hotel (now the Brindley Arms). Florence and Harold Neath kept a sweet shop in the 1950s, between the garage and the corn and seed merchants, Clarke & Crane, on the right.

An annual outing of the regulars of the Rising Sun, Lombard Street. The pub, which had its own brewhouse, was run by three generations of the Hardwick family. Thomas Horton Hardwick is on the box with Mr Hodges; his brother Harold, wearing a bowler, is on the left, near Elizabeth Hardwick their mother and the licensee. Rose Large, the maid, watches from the window.

The Railway Inn at the top of Foundry Street around 1930s. The photographer was F. Painting. Horses had to bring heavily-loaded drays up the slope past the foundry on the way to the station. St Michael's Lodge is on the near corner of Worcester Street and the Boys' School can be seen in the distance.

A tram passing cottages on the Minster Road, early 1900s. Newtown was a gem of the area's Victorian and Edwardian heritage, like the terraces of Areley Common and Wilden. The toast-rack type of tram-car was originally one of three trailer cars built for the opening of the line in 1898, and was converted with a motor one year later. The last tram between Kidderminster and Stourport ran on 2 April 1929.

The lane, now Windermere Way, around the 1930s. The lane is seen here running towards the main road, with the terraces of Lorne Street and Warwick Street on the right. Further back it became a track.

Stourport Station from the footbridge, October 1957. Loaded trucks went down the incline by gravity to the canal basin (completed 1885), where coal, iron and steel bars were loaded onto boats for Wilden Works or Stourvale. The Hartlebury to Shrewsbury line opened in 1862. The last passenger train through Stourport was on 3 January 1970.

The Red Cow Inn, Gilgal, The celebration is probably for the Coronation of George V in 1911. On the right are Tom and Louie Cox who kept the pub. The extension in front and the stable further down the road have been demolished in the recent past.

The engine station of the volunteer fire brigade, Mitton Street, in the early 1920s. When there was an emergency, Holbrooks bull (steam hooter) was blown to alert the volunteer firemen; Hodges horses had to be caught and brought, and the 'steamer' had to be fired up on the way to the fire. Before the days of the steamer, the lads of the town would follow to help with the manual pumping. Stourport Fire Brigade attended the great fire at Witley Court in 1937, and the Stourport engine was called to a fire at Hartlebury Castle on Christmas Day 1844.

An advertisement from a booklet produced by the Kidderminster & Stourport Electric Tramway Company around 1913. The Crown, the Bridge, the White Lion, the Swan and the Star are shown by name on James Sherriff's 1802 plan of Stour Port.

TELEPHONE 0199.

LION HOTEL, Stourport.

N.B.—3 Minutes' Walk from Hatton's Steamer.

THE HOUSE FOR CATERING.

Club-Room to seat 100 Persons.

Stabling for 20 Horses.

Home-Brewed Ales.

Wines and Spirits of the Finest Quality.

Don't Forget to Write and Ask for Price for YOUR Party.

S. M. GLOVER, Proprietor.

Mr and Mrs Sidney Hodges who kept the White Lion from the 1930s to the 1950s.

Armistice Day Parade, York Street, mid-1930s. Dr MacArthur from York House can be seen beyond the Fire Brigade, passing the 'white gates'.

Beach's Cycle Shop, mid 1950s. Harry Beach with his son Geoff, and grandson Don outside his first shop, which expanded into next-door premises. Harry Beach started the business from his house in Raven Street. The year 1956 marked fifty years as dealers for Raleigh.

Five
Industries

Industries along the river in the early 1950s. The canal from the industrial Midlands meets the Severn at the barge locks, where a motorboat and butty, *Nebulae*, are moored. Beyond are the gasworks (see p. 27), the vinegar brewery, and the River Stour with its past centuries of forges, mills and carpet factories. Over the Stour is the twentieth century power station.

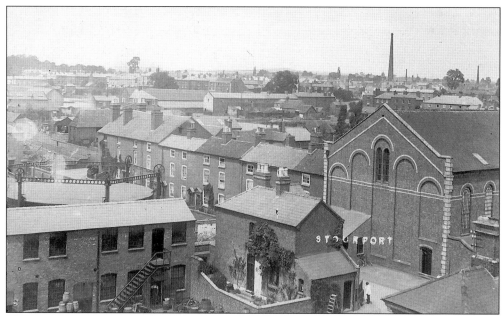

The view from the vinegar brewery, founded in 1798. Originally Swann & Co, it merged with a Birmingham brewery in 1876 and in 1900 became Holbrooks Ltd. The Sarsons name came with British Vinegars in 1954 and it was taken over by Nestlé in 1979. The photograph shows the Cheapside terrace and predates the second vat house (see below). In the foreground are the coopers' shops and the factory house, which was demolished when the new boiler house was built.

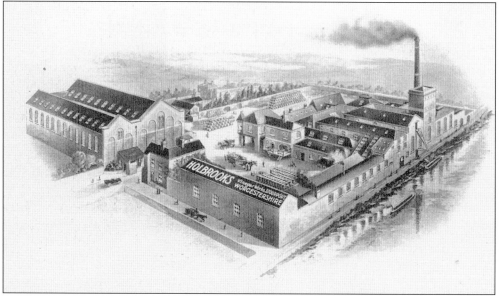

Holbrooks Vinegar Works, by a commerial artist for the 1915 price list. Though the scale is exaggerated, the layout is quite accurate and much remained in 2000, adapted alongside new facilities. The illustration shows how ingredients used to be lifted from barges on the Severn to the loading door near the water tower.

Dray near the barrel loading deck, possibly in the 1920s. There was an 'iron man', a double-rope system driven by steam engine to convey the barrels. The coopering shops and stable were later used as a fitting shop.

Demonstration by Jim Buckley, Foreman Cooper, in 1948. The series of photographs appeared in the one hundred and fiftieth anniversary issue of the Host Holbrook Bulletin. Casks were marked with the initials B.V.B.S, Birmingham Vinegar Brewery Stourport.

Stacked barrels. A water sprinkler had to be used to keep the barrels tight in the summer. The building on the left has been the Spirit House since 1960 when the spirit vinegar plant was transferred from Hull. To the right is the old bottling hall and beyond it, Stourbank House.

Holbrooks employees in 1946. In the front row from left to right: Betty Rosser, Freda Malpas, Pam Buckley, Arthur Davis, A.C. Ratcliff, F.A. Oliver, Margery Allibone, Gilbert Millis, Bill Millichip and Jim Buckley. Tony Ratcliff, the manager, wrote 'The Story of Malt Vinegar Brewing' for the one hundred and fiftieth anniversary. He was born at Stourbank House and was the son of F.D. Ratcliff, who became manager in 1911.

The opening of the new building in 1988. The new amenity block, laboratory, bottling hall and production office was opened by Baroness Trumpington, Parliamentary Secretary at the Ministry of Agriculture, Fisheries and Food. Barrie Gould, manager from 1968-1994, is showing her coopering tools, which are now at the County Museum, Hartlebury. Since 1997 soy sauce has been produced in the new building.

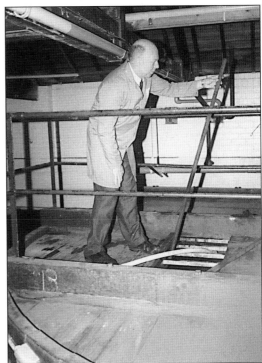

Paul Brazier, technical leader, with the last vat of Worcester Sauce. The mechanical stirrer of vat forty-nine was turned off on 3 April 2000. This is one of a set of photographs by M.B. Nagington.

Paul Brazier in the spirit house, April 2000, after brewing had ceased. This is the hall on the east side (see p. 70), containing eleven spirit acetifiers for making spirit vinegar. Two of the 50,000 gallon vats in the hall to the west date from 1912. An auctioneer's label on the left heralds the end of over 200 years of vinegar brewing at Stourport.

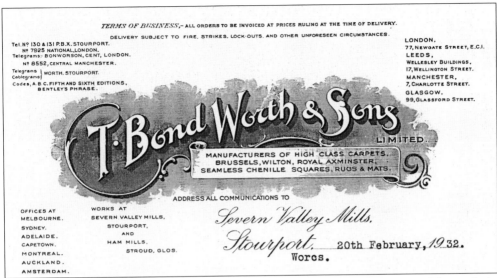

TERMS OF BUSINESS,- ALL ORDERS TO BE INVOICED AT PRICES RULING AT THE TIME OF DELIVERY.
DELIVERY SUBJECT TO FIRE, STRIKES, LOCK-OUTS, AND OTHER UNFORESEEN CIRCUMSTANCES.

Tel. Nº 130 & 131 P.B.X. STOURPORT.
Nº 7925 NATIONAL, LONDON.
Telegrams: BONWORSON, CENT, LONDON.
Nº 8552, CENTRAL MANCHESTER.
Telegrams } WORTH, STOURPORT.
Cablegrams }
Codes, A.B.C. FIFTH AND SIXTH EDITIONS,
BENTLEYS PHRASE.

LONDON,
77, NEWGATE STREET, E.C.I.
LEEDS,
WELLESLEY BUILDINGS,
17, WELLINGTON STREET.
MANCHESTER,
7, CHARLOTTE STREET.
GLASGOW,
99, GLASSFORD STREET.

T. Bond Worth & Sons LIMITED.

MANUFACTURERS OF HIGH CLASS CARPETS,
BRUSSELS, WILTON, ROYAL AXMINSTER,
SEAMLESS CHENILLE SQUARES, RUGS & MATS.

ADDRESS ALL COMMUNICATIONS TO

OFFICES AT
MELBOURNE.
SYDNEY.
ADELAIDE.
CAPETOWN.
MONTREAL.
AUCKLAND.
AMSTERDAM.

WORKS AT
SEVERN VALLEY MILLS,
STOURPORT,
AND
HAM MILLS,
STROUD, GLOS.

Severn Valley Mills.
Stourport,   20th February, 1932.
Worcs.

The fine engraved letterhead of T. Bond Worth in 1932. (See p. 25 for a view of the works in 1933.) Thomas Bond Worth's original factory, the Severn Valley Mills, was built about 1866 for the newly introduced power looms. In the early years several carpet manufacturers used the buildings. The site was further developed by T. Bond Worth & Sons in the late 1800s and in the 1920s, with characteristic design of the period. The company became Carpets of Worth Ltd under new ownership in 1979.

The carpet works seen from the garden of Lichfield House, home of Thomas Bond Worth (born 1833) and his wife Eliza, née Baldwin, possibly in the 1880s.

75

The old entrance, Severn Valley Mills, probably in the 1880s. It once led to the Canal Company's old engine building on the Stour. The field on the right was developed in the late 1920s. A large new shed, 'Germany', was built for seamless Axminster and Wilton looms.

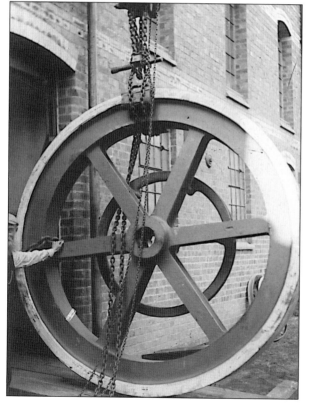

Believed to be the flywheel for the first mill engine. It was manufactured by Worth Mackenzie of Darlington. On the left is their consulting engineer, Robert Worth, 1845-1916, younger brother of Thomas Bond Worth, who came down to see it installed.

Celebration in Worth's picking room at the end of the First World War. Leonora Shellis is on the fourth table back.

Bantocks dray in Severn Road outside Bond Worth's loading bay, in the 1940s (see p. 96). The head office of Thomas Bantock & Co, carriers, was at Wolverhampton; Mr Bantock's house in Wolverhampton is now a museum. Their agent at Stourport station was Mr Harold E. Poole.

Bill Jones and Bernard Pritchett in the boiler house at Bond Worth, 1949.

Bond Worth ladies cricket team in front of the pavilion at the sports ground, Mill Road, around 1938. From left to right, back row: Lil Dubber, Aline Stone, -?-, Gwen Mace, Ruby Wilde. Front row: Val Bailey, Edna Heybeard, Edna Dorrell, Elsie Watkins, Gwen Bayliss, Stella Puplett.

The tannery around 1920, taken before the construction of Vale Road. Following a great fire about 1860, Joseph and John Crane Rogers rebuilt the tannery in grand style with a 200ft chimney. In 1880, Henry Hall Beakbane took over the tannery, the wharf, sixteen cottages and the Heath. The tannery was restructured on a reduced site about 1910. It was again destroyed by fire on 10 July 1964. The photograph shows clearly the old route from Mitton Gardens.

Thomas Vale workers, Lickhill Road, 1930. Vales' offices were the former tannery manager's house in Lombard Street. Thomas Vale Construction celebrated one hundred and twenty-five years in 1994, adopting a new logo recalling their founder's part in building Stourport Bridge. Vales were the builders of the Drill Hall, 1911.

A promotional engraving of the foundry. The canal side office building, now listed, is the only survivor of this busy scene stretching from the tannery on the left to the Boys' School on the right. Baldwins cast iron butt hinges were exported worldwide. The foundry ceased production on 27 January 1956.

The casting shop at the foundry, around 1930. From left to right, back row: Harry Morris, Bill Richards, Freddie Wall, Cyril Jones, George Richards, Bonny Richards, Len Southall. Middle row: Ted Lippett, -?-, Ralph Southall, Jim Thomas, Cliff Birch, Gil Jones, Ike Nunney. Sitting: Harry Holloway, George Large, Harry Large, Charlie Bath, Len Lashford, Tom Lashford, Alf Cooper, -?-.

The enamelling section of Anglo Enamelware in Baldwin Road. On the left is Enoch Baldwin, third from left is Frank Goode who worked in the time office, to the left of the entrance. The Anglo closed in March 1957.

Match case presented to guests at the official opening of the Electric Power House on 2 June 1927 by the Rt Hon. Stanley Baldwin, Prime Minister. The enterprise of the Power Company caused Steatite and Porcelain Products Ltd, manufacturer of insulators and a major electricity user, to be sited in Stourport. (see p. 83)

A group of workmates at the power station, 1931-1932. Among them are Stanley Shimmin, a welder who was seconded from the Isle of Man; Ernie Ward and Jack Barnes.

On the branch line at the power station, around 1968. The locomotive, Peckett W/No 1893, went into service at Ironbridge Power Station in 1936 and came to Stourport from Birchills. Two battery-powered locomotives, obtained in 1925, had been used on the narrow-gauge line from Severn Road for coal brought by canal. Construction of the branch line started in 1940 and coal transport by canal ceased around 1949.

Arthur Smith working at the control panel for B1 turbine and boiler, around 1968. B Station was opened in September 1950. The power station closed in 1984.

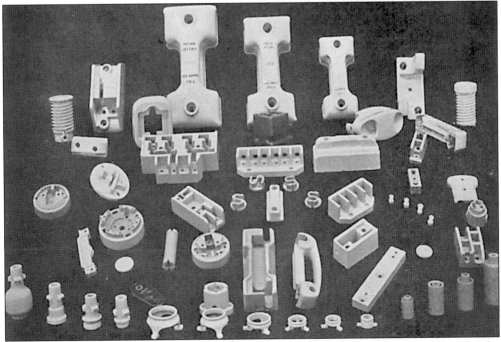

Low tension pressed goods produced in 1930 by Steatite and Porcelain Products Ltd. The company built the factory in Stourport in 1929. It had the latest amenities and new housing to which families moved from the depressed areas of South Wales. The company is now known as Morgan Advanced Ceramics, formerly Morgan Matroc.

A bank of automatic presses for steatite, 1930. The dry pressed goods were then packed into saggars, round fire-clay containers, and carried by conveyor to the tunnel kiln for firing. The steelwork of the building was painted in white enamel to maintain extreme cleanliness for the production process.

Ted Hodgkiss, Lloydy Williams, Len Such and Levi Dean with high voltage ceramic insulator bushes. The insulators were used on power station equipment.

Testing ceramic insulators in the high-tension laboratory, 1950s. The flashover appears as a diaphanous web of electricity. The specially reinforced laboratory, which was demolished in 1994, created extreme climatic conditions for testing electrical and mechanical properties.

Parsons Chain celebrated its centenary in 2003. In 1902 Harry Parsons, an engineer with the City and Suburban Electric Carriage Company Ltd in London, took out a patent for a 'non-skidder' at a time of burgeoning developments in pioneer motoring. A company was formed to cut and assemble non-skid chains. Its success, particularly in America, led to purchase in 1915 by a company which became the American Chain and Cable Co. In 1924 British Wire products was purchased as a subsidiary and in 1931 the company started to manufacture chain, shipping equipment from America to premises in Stourport, close to the Midlands industries they supplied. It is said that the quality of the fishing might just possibly have influenced the final choice of Stourport for the new venture. In the 1930s, the company began supplying chains to the mining industry. During the Second World War heavy, non-skid chains were produced for military vehicles in the desert. Through technological development, the company expanded to export to all the major countries of the world, supplying chain equipment for heavy industry, mining, fishing and sugar cane transportation.

A Parsons Chain Kuplex Lifting Sling in use, about 1962. A 25T ingot in 18/23 mild steel is being off loaded with the sling at Folkes Forge Ltd on the Stourport Road.

Two
Schools

Basketmaking at Tan Lane School, 1912. The teacher is Miss Weeks and the photograph shows the gallery, which seemed so high to children at the time. At the front are Nora and Rose Stokes.

A class at Tan Lane School, 1931. The school's foundation stone was laid in 1892 and the building was in use by 1894. The school celebrated its centenary in 1997, from the date its logbooks started. From left to right, front row: Audrey Cooper, Joyce Stokes, Kath Carradine, Joan Perry, Milly Slater. Second row: Edna Barratt, Violet Round, Brenda Rogers, Evelyn Tallboys, -?-, Joyce Wood, Doris Robinson, Ethel Wassell. Third row: ? James, Muriel Mayall, Joyce Clarke, Mary Nash, Lorna Baggot, Kathleen Callow, Hilda Leek, Joan Badham, Nora Jones. Back row: Maisie Moule, Jean Hodges, Sheila Belcher, Muriel Marks, Frances Ibbotson, Graham Neal, Phyllis Thompson, Gloria Grinnall, Eunice Knight.

Two classes at Areley Kings School, probably photographed in 1928 or 1929. The teacher on the left is Miss Farmer and on the right is the headmaster Mr Gill, who later became a master at Stourport County Senior School, 'the school in the Park'.

Children from St John's Church of England School on Minster Road, at the Heath in 1937. The girls' red, white and blue paper dresses were in honour of the Coronation of King George VI. Brenda Poole was in this group, photographed by her sister. Mr and Mrs Capel Loft opened their grounds for many social occasions of that time. The Heath was formerly the residence of the Rogers (see p. 51) and later the Beakbanes, owners of the tannery.

Class three at the Girls' School, Church Avenue, in 1931. Among the group are Helen Morgan, Evelyn Buckley, Madeline Beach and Grace Knight. The home of Mrs Jinks, the caretaker, is on the left. The school was built in 1842 and enlarged in 1887.

Stourport Boys' School about 1927. The group is taken in the playground, which was on the other side of the Bewdley Road. On the left is the headmaster, George Gregory, who was in St Michael's church choir. His brother Roland, also a teacher at the school, was the organist. On the right is Mr R. Cook from Kidderminster. The grounds of The Firs are in the background. Bill Bullock, second from right in the third row back, trained with the gardener at Moor Hall and ran the Heath Nurseries in Lickhill Road, started by his father in 1913. He was first elected chairman of Stourport UDC in 1957.

The Boy's School, seen from a garden in Vernon Road, mid 1930s. This worn snapshot is one of the few known photographs of the 'Bombed Boys School' (see p. 104). The small child is Walter Millward.

Staff of the Stourport County Senior School when it opened in 1936. It was only the second of its type in the county. The newly appointed headmaster Mr E.J. Jones, 1936-1962, set about purchasing equipment for the school and discovered that schools in the county were strictly forbidden to purchase a wireless in that comparatively new age of radio. The custom ended there and then for Stourport. From left to right, back row: Mr W.H. Gill, Mr R.J. Clarke, Mr Hanglin, Miss M. Kirkman, Mr Clay, Mr T.E. Merriman, Mr B. Jones. Front row: Miss Elcock, Miss Joslin, Miss Hardwick, Mr Jones, Miss Burberry, Miss V.A. Fathers, Miss Thomas.

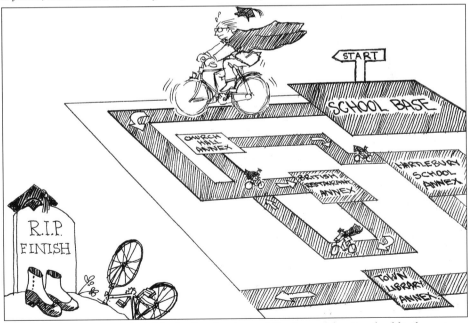

One of the brilliant cartoons by Malcolm Brookes in a publication celebrating the fiftieth anniversary of Stourport-on-Severn High School in 1986. Mr Jones, in his spats, is seen dashing between the wartime annexes of the school. The move to the new school on the Minster Road started in 1954.

Girls from Stourport Senior School on a trip to London in April 1949. Standing in front of the war-damaged façade of the Science Museum are, from left to right, back row: Doreen Hutton, Daphne Jones, Iris Powell, Miss Webster, Gillian Tustin, Judith Forty, Mrs Preston, Pauline Goodwin. Front row: Sheila Cox, Margaret Shimmin, Sheila Husselbee, Betty Barten, Jacqueline Gardner.

Senior School boys in Trafalgar Square, 1951. As the famous emblem shows, they were on a trip to see the Festival of Britain at the South Bank.

Seven
Wartime

A whist drive for convalescent servicemen during the First World War. It was held at Concordia, Church Avenue, the home of Mr and Mrs George Jackson. Mr Jackson was headmaster of the Boys' School from 1883-1924. The mansion across Church Avenue was the vicarage, once called Belle Vue. It was listed, but permission was given to demolish it in 1969.

The Drill Hall, Lion Hill. It was opened by the Earl of Dudley on 30 December 1911, and was soon to be involved in the dark years of the First World War. The occasion and date of this rare photograph are unknown. The facilities of the Drill Hall included the residence for the sergeant-instructor, who was for many years Isaac Nunney. The local council in 1952-1953 acquired the walled premises opposite from British Waterways and created the gardens, for which stonework was bought from Witley Court.

The Victorian residence next to the windmill at Areley Kings was used as a Red Cross Hospital in the First World War. It was later the home of Dr Stanley Robinson and finally the Severn Manor Hotel. Records of Holbrooks show that they, and no doubt other companies in the town, contributed weekly to wartime causes such as the French Relief Fund, Stourport Red Cross Hospital, Kidderminster Infirmary, British Ambulance Committee, Verdun Refugees and Cigarettes to Employees at the Front.

Staff and convalescents at the Red Cross Hospital.

Unveiling the 1914-1918 war memorial in the High Street, April 1922. Mr Stanley (later Earl) Baldwin MP contributed £500 towards the memorial, which was made by the Bromsgrove Guild. The memorial was on the boundary of Bank House garden but was moved around 1977 to the corner of Vale Road and Mitton Street. The Central Garage can be seen in the background, to the left of the Wheatsheaf brewhouse.

Putting lids on grenades on a conveyor belt at Bond Worth. During the Second World War, the factory was used by the Admiralty for storage and by Albright & Wilson of Oldbury to produce anti-tank bombs and grenades. If they became contaminated by phosphorus, workers had to plunge into the emergency bath.

Worths Home Guard about 1941. From left to right, back row: Arthur Cox, Ernie Knight, Jack Bourne, Jack Wild, Harold Francis. Middle row: Bernard Pritchett, who was awarded the Distinguished Conduct Medal in the First World War, Bill Herbert, Charlie Mace, Len Southall, Len Rowley. Front row: Trevor Philips, Doug Currell, Maurice Southall, Charlie Ingram. Holbrooks and Stourbank House are in the background.

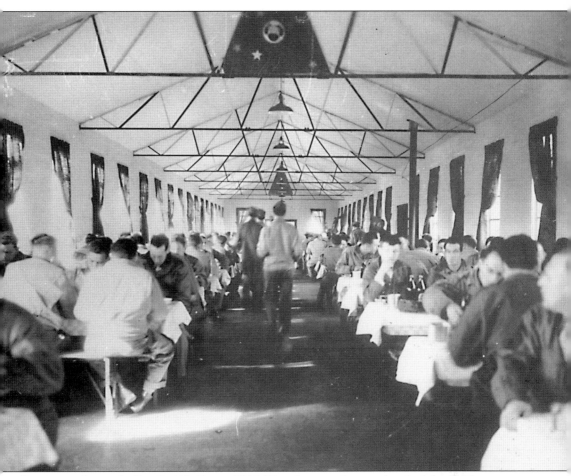

Servicemen's mess hall at Burlish Camp, 1944. The photograph was taken by John P. Thomson, who was Communications Sergeant at the 297th American General Hospital. An American army camp, using concrete prefab and timber buildings, had been set up in 1942, covering part of the present Burlish Park Estate as well as Burlish Top and as far as Birchen Coppice Estate. After the mass departure of the troops, the camp was converted in three weeks to receive battle casualties, who were brought in hospital trains from Southampton. Ambulances went in convoys to transport the wounded from the station. There were two hospital units, the 297th on Windermere Way and the 114th on Burlish Top, each accommodating 1,442 patients. By VE Day, over 12,000 casualties had been received at the hospital. At the end of the war, it was used as a rehabilitation centre for American POWs. The British Army then used the huts to house the Education Corps and Pioneer Corps. In the aftermath of the war there was a severe housing shortage across the country, and some local people and families from Birmingham moved into the vacant huts as squatters. In 1949 Stourport Urban District Council took on administration of the camp buildings and put in bathrooms and kitchens for their tenants. Some of the housing was allocated to refugees from Eastern Europe; a building beside Kingsway was converted as a church for the Polish residents. People speak with pleasure of their time living in the converted huts of Burlish Camp after the war. The camp was eventually run down and closed in the late 1950s, but traces of its history remain among the paths of the Burlish Top Nature Reserve.

At the Town Hall, women sewing for the war effort. Among the group are Mrs Osborne, Mrs Roberts, Mrs Joyner, Mrs Belcher, and Mrs Wilkes working the treadle machine. The children are Bobby Jones and Margaret Roberts. In peacetime the Town Hall, like the Drill Hall, was the venue for dances, concerts and other social events. During the war, civil defence supplies were kept there and at the old bank buildings.

The Stourport Home Guard Band outside the Drill Hall. The band was formed from the old Stourport Town Band. J. Namashack, centre with the clarinet, came from the US Army Nursing Section in Vale Road to play with the band. Fred Bevan is next to him on the right.

Steatite's Home Guard at Witley Court around 1940-1941. From left to right, back row: Tom Gough, Tom Knight, Jim Clutterbuck, Bill Tipper, Les Comley, Cyril Brown, Bill Allman. Middle row: Frank Cox, Bert Morris, Walter Slater, Bill Harris, Joe Shaw, Eli Thomas. Front row: Sid Cook, Colin Clark, Geoff Halton, Dick Comber, Hans Kuestner, George Slater, Cyril Storey. Mr Halton became managing director in 1955.

End of the war: Victory parade up the High Street, headed by the Home Guard Band. The old post office of 1901, replaced in 1964, can be seen on the right.

Party in the Lion Yard at the end of the war. Mr and Mrs Hodges of the Lion, sitting at the head of the table, had organized the party and provided the lemonade. The children had to collect their ration of two artificial-cream cakes from Wimbushes in the High Street. After tea, there were games; three-legged and sack races in the brick-paved yard. Memories are of a wartime community which consisted mainly of women, children and the older generation.

Eight
Events and Organizations

Stourport Power Station Sports Club Band, 1950s. Here we have Clarence Cook on saxophone, Bert Such on drums, Stan Shimmin on trumpet and Les Bowen on piano. The first three were members of the Stourport Town Band.

Members of the great Stourport musical family, the Evers, giving a performance probably at Witley Court. Ben Evers is playing the cello, accompanied by his daughter Gertrude, a fine contralto singer, who married L.W. Southall in 1915. Her versatile talents included playing the piano for silent films at Stourport Electric Theatre.

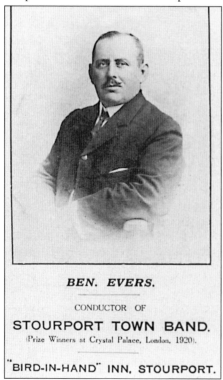

BEN. EVERS.

CONDUCTOR OF

STOURPORT TOWN BAND.

(Prize Winners at Crystal Palace, London, 1920).

"BIRD-IN-HAND" INN, STOURPORT.

Ben Evers, a fine cornetist, was licensee of the Bird-in-Hand where he founded the famous Town Band in 1901, with the help of his sons who played cornet, euphonium, clarinet, trombone and French horn. He built a band room for practice at the 'Bird' and they had a floating bandstand for music on the river. They won national awards at Crystal Palace and Belle Vue, Manchester, and the band remained in existence for over fifty years.

Stourport Town Band in the Memorial Park in the late 1920s. Stanley Baldwin, MP and Prime Minister, centre, was president of the band from its start until his death in 1947. Fred Bevan, in the back row, fourth from left, is next to his father Walter, both clarinettists. Ben Evers, sitting next to Tommy Dunn's bass drum, has four sons in this photograph.

Royal Silver Jubilee celebrations, 6 May 1935. Stourport '-on-Severn', its newly extended name, celebrated George V's Jubilee with Thanksgiving Services, children's teas, sports and music in the Memorial Park, an illuminated river parade, fireworks and a beacon on Stagborough Hill. Here the Stourport Town Prize Band is heading the Church Parade Procession out of New Street followed by detachments of the 7th Battalion Worcestershire Regiment.

Silver Jubilee decorations in Worcester Street. The street was renowned for its communal displays and these Jubilee decorations attracted more than one photographer. This view shows the Boys' School, which was hit by a chance bomb dropped five years later one Sunday in November. The terrace of cottages had long gardens running back to Bewdley Road, near the junction with Foundry Street.

The Electric Theatre, in Lickhill Road, later the Haven Cinema, decorated for the Jubilee. The cinema is believed to be one of the oldest in the country, possibly dating from around 1908. This little snapshot shows Miss Betty Sutton (Mrs J.W. Bullock), who sold the tickets, and John Courtney Powell, the manager, who was also the Urban District Council Rating Officer and a coal merchant.

Hughes Stationers, No. 3 High Street, decorated for George VI's coronation on 12 May 1937.
Posing with their magnificent displays are Miss Edna Hughes and Miss Iris Mills.

A street party in Prospect Road to celebrate Queen Elizabeth II's coronation on 2 June 1953.
Molly Roberts, Ada Harmer, Ivy Carter and Con Pickering are helping to serve out the teas.

The Royal Party arriving by train for the first Stourport Carnival, 2 June 1925. The train from Hartlebury puffed into Stourport station the wrong way round and was greeted by a fanfare from the amazed Town Band, as Ben Evers, centre, and Ernest Millner, right, descended from the train with Len Southall, left, Mary Southall and her cousin Peggy Evers. Their grandfather, Ben Evers, senior, was knighted as Master of the Musique and the party set off by horse and carriage round the town. The royal costumes had been hired in London where Ben Evers, junior, played at the Savoy Hotel.

In 1932 the 'Stourport Royal Carnival' had as its patrons the Duke of York, the Bishop of Worcester and Stanley Baldwin MP. Isaac Nunney was marshall of the parade. The crowning of the Carnival Queen took place at the bandstand in the Memorial Park. Entertainments in the park included selections played by the Town Band, a bowling competition, grand boxing displays, a jazz band contest, dancing displays, and Punch and Judy. There was also 'freak bowling' for a live pig. On the river, the houseboats, rafts, bungalows, club boathouse and bridge were illuminated and the 'Sydney Glover' Cup went to the best illuminated craft. Prizes in twenty-five classes were presented at the Drill Hall six days later, followed by the dance (in carnival dress) to Mr Turner's Dance Band. In the 1934 'Land & Water Carnival' you could have a sixpenny trip up the river on the hydroglider, Scorpion, and there were also rowing and swimming events. The Townswomen's Guild Choir and the Town Band gave a musical interlude from Captain Palmer's SS Princess Beatrice.

Carnival procession, Mitton Street, in 1925. The cottages on the right, from the corner of Severn Road and down Stour Lane, were demolished for Bond Worth's new buildings. The pub in the distance is the Crown and Anchor.

The Carnival Queen and her Maids of Honour, 15 July 1933. Pictured at the bandstand in the Memorial Park is Molly Yardley, and with her, from left to right: Phyllis Whitmore, Phyllis Baylis, Frances Waring and Mabel Oakes. Among the dignitaries are Dr Brocket of Oakleigh, Councillor Bullus and Isaac Nunney from the Drill Hall.

The Sea Cadets' pirate boat in the Carnival River Parade about 1947. The Sea Cadets' entry, seen here in front of Stourport Boat Club, was towed by Harry Prescott's boat 'Mimic'. Daphne Moone (née Prescott) remembers that she finished up off the gang plank in the river at least twice.

Parsons Chain carnival float, Alice in Wonderland, at the assembly point by the Memorial Park around the mid-1950s. From left to right: Brenda Poole, Iris Langford, Margaret Hill, Sheila Guest, Mary Davis and Bella Moule. The driver is Mr Dyson.

An Edwardian regatta. Areley Kings church is just off to the left. The first open regatta was held in the 1860s. Before Stourport Boat Club's boathouse was built in 1901, a converted trow with a floating landing stage was used. The progress and successes of rowing at Stourport are colourfully described by I.L. Wedley in his series of *Kidderminster Shuttle* articles of 1934. Stourport Regatta from 1980-1988 was claimed to be the largest in the country and in 1994 Stourport became the most successful rowing club in the UK, with 120 wins in open events.

Stourport Junior Crew passing the Tontine. They were the winners of the Evesham Challenge Vase, 1925, and were E. Wright, H. Hibberd, L.A. Ward, A.C. Griffiths and the cox, J. Cope.

Stourport Townswomen's Guild at the old Town Hall around 1950. Seated in the centre is Mrs Roland Worth, president of the Guild, with her daughter-in-law, Mrs Edward Worth, on the left, and Mrs Len Southall (Gertrude Evers p. 102) who was chairman, on the right. From left to right, back row: Mrs Wilcox, Mrs Kidley, Mrs Yates, Mrs Wilkes, Miss Welsh, Mrs Gilbert, Mrs Nightingale, Mrs Hancox, Mrs Armstrong, Mrs Comley, Miss Armstrong and Miss Lizzie Chell.

Parade down Lichfield Street to the British Legion, 1948. The Primitive Methodists were fundraising for their new church, Vernon Hall, which celebrated its fiftieth anniversary in 1999. Harold Reynolds was Father Christmas, accompanying Patricia Davies and Hilda Leek. John Bone was at the head of the Sea Cadets and Ted Millward, then *Shuttle* reporter, can be seen in the following crowd.

The Stourport Veterans in the early to mid 1950s. Pictured in front of their building in the park are: from left to right, back row: Arthur Ricketts, James Stokes, Charles Hardwick, Tommy Dunn, Bill Higgins. Middle row: Jack Kirk, Jim Lashford, -?-, -?-, Fred Hutton, Harry Neal, Frank Osbourne, Tom Lashford, Mr Williams. Front row: Mr Millward, George Southall, Ted Cox, Walter Bevan, Dan Greenwood, Bill Bloor, George Phillips, Mr Millichip, George Marks. Cyril Lashford ran activities for the Veterans. They had a library and events such as whist drives, trips on the river and other outings.

'A souvenir of a Great Occasion', 1948. The team from the First Stourport St Michael's Scout Troop won the Oldnall Cup competition for a weekend's hiking. From left to right, standing: Jacky Malpas, John Shuter, Cyril Arnold, Alan Millington and Peter Griffiths. Front row: Brian Parker, Maurice Rowles and Michael Bourne. The old houses in the background were between Vale Road and the canal. The photograph was taken by Arthur Worth, who treated the team to a supper of faggots and peas at the Bridge Café.

The Stourport Swifts and West Bromwich Albion teams outside the Red Lion around 1933. The Swifts played on ground where Parsons Chain later extended their works, and the team changed at the Red Lion, now known as the Steps. West Bromwich Albion came to play Stourport Swifts for some seasons in the early 1930s to raise funds. This followed the signing of Ted Crowe, the Swifts goalkeeper. He was taken to the Albion by the ex-England International left back, Jesse Pennington, who lived in the Stourport area. The Swifts team here includes goalkeeper Gerry Clissett, Alec Adams, Charlie Bourne, Bert Guest, Cyril Bloor, Teddy Thomas, Bill Thomas, with trainer Mr Crowther. At the back are Harry Boulton, Ernie Dunne, Mr Greenwood, Jim Lashford, Councillor Bullus, Wallie Foster, George Evans and in the bowler hat, Ben Evers, whose pub, the Bird-in-Hand, was the great centre of West Bromwich Albion support in Stourport at that time.

Stourport Cricket Club in the Memorial Park, 1938. The occasion was a challenge match between the First and Second Elevens. From left to right, front row: Frank Evans, Marjorie Stokes, Carol Wooley, Gladys Whitefoot, Vic Tallboys. Middle row: Bill Millner, Geoff Nunney, Geoff Darby, Jack Stringer, Ken Bourne, Harry Whitefoot, Fred Mountford, Reg Evans. Back row: George Wainwright, Jim Whitmore, Bob Wainwright, Dick Stringer, Jack Shellis, Reg Walters, Harry Mountford, E. Hughes, F. McCulloch, Bill Evans, Arthur Stokes, Mrs Nunney, Les Nunney, Bill Gent.

A combined bowling clubs team at Hagley Hall in the 1930s. A team was selected annually by Harry Neal, captain of the champion Brinton Arms Bowling Club, to play against the Worcestershire Gentlemen. The group posing with Lord Cobham includes Mr Hutton, Ben and Harry Evers, Mr Phipps, Harry Neal, Jack Sanger, Hubert Ayres, Bert Whatmore, Mr Fewtrell and Harry Bennett. Many Stourport pubs had bowling greens and they were kept to a high standard.

The Royal Oak Fishing Club, Severn Road (see p.27). Harry Buckley, who worked at the canal maintenance yard and built the ice boat in 1930, is holding the cup. He learnt boat building from his father-in-law, James Baldwin (who had taken over the first boat raft on the river, started by his father, John).

The Squirrel Darts Team and supporters, 1938. The team, posing with Mrs Connie Sutton the licensee, are Jack Butler, Harry Bullimore, Jack Large, Arthur Gregory the captain, Jack Preece, Horace Haywood, Ted Wilkes, Percy Ravenhill and Robin Preece.

Nine
People and Places

The Harrisons at tea around 1915. (See p. 123). Walter Harrison (1852-1945), his wife Henriette, their daughter Christine, and an unknown friend. At about this time, their eldest son Julius, the composer, conducted for Sir Thomas Beecham's newly-founded Beecham Opera Company at the Shaftesbury Theatre in London.

Moorhill (later called Moor Hall), a drawing from a contemporary watercolour. *The Cambrian Traveller's Guide* in 1813 called it 'a new mansion, the residence of Jonathan Worthington Esq.' As the sale details of 1844 show, it was a most beautiful house, situated in fine grounds, with 'hot and green houses' and vistas over the landscape to the south and west.

Sarah (1769-1796), the first wife of Jonathan Worthington. She was the younger daughter of Aaron York, wharfinger, of York House, and married in 1789. Sarah died aged twenty-seven, soon after her fifth child was born. Aaron York died three months later, having lost his only son and Sarah within three years.

Jonathan Worthington 1756-1821. He was the son of a road carrier at Old Trafford and went into business as a canal carrier with John Gilbert, based at Manchester and transporting on the newly-opened route to Stourport. He married into the York family in Stourport and the carrying companies of York and Worthington eventually merged after the death of John Gilbert in 1812.

Richard Jukes, 1768-1834, portrait by Thomas Phillips RA. Richard Jukes, originally from Cound in Shropshire, was surgeon apothecary in Stourport and was in partnership with Kenrick Watson. His sister Elizabeth was the second wife of Jonathan Worthington; they married in 1802. Jukes and Watson forwarded the career of their gifted apprentice, Charles Hastings, who was with them from 1810-1812. He went on to found the British Medical Association and was subsequently knighted, (see p. 56).

The title-page from George Nicholson's 'Conduct of Man', fourth edition, the first being from Manchester in 1797. The frontispiece illustrates the story of a Norfolk farmer saved by his dog when he collapsed in the bitter frost of 1794-1795.

George Nicholson (1760-1825), who came from a Yorkshire printing background, became himself a celebrated printer, author and bookseller, establishing his countrywide reputation from a number of bases, in Bradford, Manchester, Ludlow, and Poughnill in Shropshire, before setting up at Stourport in 1808 (see p. 53). He was immensely industrious, producing an astounding number of book titles and subjects, some as part of his famous collection, 'The Literary Miscellany; or Selections & Extracts, Classical and Scientific', others in an innovative tiny pocket-book series. A local boy who later became MP for Worcester, Thomas Rowley Hill, 'distinctly remembered him as a tall, gaunt man. He was an author and printed chiefly by his own hands. He was a great scientific crony of my Father.' He chose a Spartan life-style apparently, was a staunch vegetarian, and was an early, dedicated campaigner against animal cruelties and sports.

His extensive prefaces to whatever the work in hand show Nicholson to be a zealous educator, likely to be seen offering advice to all and sundry on most topics. The two editions in 1808 and 1813 of 'The Cambrian Traveller's Guide' to Wales and the Marches, probably his widest-known compilation, covered not only topography but flora and fauna in great detail. He personally walked over a large part of the region, so could prescribe the right care of the feet and the correct form of footwear. Clearly the town thought well of him, for his memorial in St Michael's churchyard reads in part, 'a man of strict integrity and a warm advocate of humanity.'

Conservatory of Moor Hall, early 1900s. Moor Hall (see p. 116) was sold by J. Worthington, son, in 1844. By 1868 it was the residence of the carpet manufacturer, John Brinton JP and later, MP. He considerably enlarged and altered the house and estate in the Victorian manner.

J.H. Wilson, gardener, in the greenhouses at Moor Hall. Another family photograph shows prizewinning black grapes from Moor Hall, Shrewsbury Floral Fete, 1907. John Brinton died in 1914 and in June 1917 Moor Hall was put up for sale at the Grand Hotel, Birmingham.

Wilden House, home of the ironfounding magnate and MP, Alfred Baldwin, taken from a card posted in 1923. The early Victorian house was much extended by Alfred Baldwin after he moved there in 1870. It was the childhood home of Stanley Baldwin from the age of three. The contents of the house were auctioned after the death of the last resident, Edith Macdonald, and it was demolished in 1939 to allow for road widening.

Stanley Baldwin in the top garden at Wilden House, a painting by Philip Burne-Jones his cousin, around 1886. The chimneys of Baldwins Wilden works are seen below. Stanley Baldwin worked there for twenty years as a partner in the business.

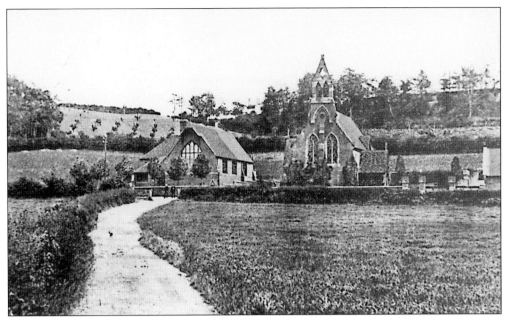

Wilden church and school, a view of 1906 or earlier. All Saints church was built by Alfred Baldwin and is famed for its stained glass windows, designed by Edward Burne-Jones. The church (1880), school (1882), gatehouse and clock memorial (1910) are all of a piece and influenced by the Baldwins' family connections with the arts world of the time.

War Memorial Park, a card posted in 1935. On the bank is the Lucy Baldwin Maternity Home, opened on 15 April 1929 by Stanley Baldwin. It was a gift to Mrs Baldwin from a Nottingham philanthropist, Mr Julian Cahn, in response to her appeal in *The Times*. It was intended as a 'pioneer home of similar homes that would spread all through the country'.

Isaac Wedley at the Laurels, Lickhill Road. I.L. Wedley, 1865-1941, photographer, musician, local historian and journalist, made an incomparable record of early twentieth century Stourport. He was the local reporter for the *Kidderminster Shuttle* and also Registrar of Births and Deaths. The Wedleys' house, The Laurels, was opposite Heath Lodge. Many Methodist church events were held in their garden. He taught the piano (his concert grand is in the photograph), violin and cello. He was the organist and choirmaster of the Wesleyan Methodist church for fifty years, and cycled all around the Marches and Wales, from church to church, to play the organs. His photographs have a quality of their own which brings the era to life. His son, Geoff, was also a fine photographer and musician.

Much of the history of Stourport and handed-down memories of the town are amassed in his writings, *'Old Stourport'*, 1912, *'The Passing of Mitton'* 1921, *'Twixt Severn and Teme'* 1928, articles of 1933-5: *'Stourport, Its Rise, Decline and Final Triumph '*, and more. His brother, John, wrote *'The History of Methodism in the Stourport Circuit'* 1899.

A story is told that Isaac Wedley once hired a rowing boat at Stourport, rowed down to Gloucester and there rode the Severn Bore in it.

Julius Harrison, composer and conductor, 1885-1963. He was the eldest son of Walter H. Harrison, who had gone into his father's grocery business at No. 11 York Street, and was a founder member of Stourport Boat Club, a keen cricketer, and above all, a musician and singer. Walter Harrison organised the Stourport Glee Union, with whom Edward Elgar sometimes played violin. He married Henriette Schoeller from Heidelberg, also a gifted musician, and the family were given a richly musical background. They lived for a while in the 1890s at No. 4 Lichfield Street, and attended the school of the Misses Mary and Nelly Broad, two doors away. They then lived over the shop in York Street, which had a monkey-puzzle tree in the yard, and stable and warehouse behind.

Father and sons sang in Wilden church choir, along with Stanley Baldwin. Julius attended Hartlebury Grammar School and had a job as organist at Areley Kings church at the age of sixteen. Years later, Dr Robinson of York House wrote to his fellow Old Elizabethans of how Julius's practising had kept him awake to the early hours, 'until the lark in the cage next door was about to start'. In 1903 Julius had a scholarship to the Birmingham & Midland Institute and it was during that time that he first met Edward Elgar, who was delivering a series of lectures at the Institute. Julius Harrison returned for five years as organist and choirmaster of Hartlebury church.

Many of his subsequent works as a composer were influenced by his love of Worcestershire. The movements of his *Worcestershire Suite* include an evocation of Redstone Rock and the Shrawley Round and the memory of a roistering song at the Bridge Inn. He had a distinguished career as a conductor, founded the Elgar Festival at Malvern, and in later life produced his two greatest works, 'Mass in C', and 'Requiem'. 'Requiem' was a tribute for the centenary of Elgar's birth; it was first performed at the Three Choirs Festival at Worcester in 1957. Forty years earlier, during the First World War, he had conducted the first performance of Elgar's music for 'The Starlight Express' at the Kingsway in London.

A special occasion for Stourport was a prestigious concert at the Drill Hall in April 1920, by the Stourport Choral Society. In the programme was the first performance of a work written for them and conducted by Julius Harrison. A new work by the local composer, Easthope Martin, was also performed. The organist was Isaac Wedley.

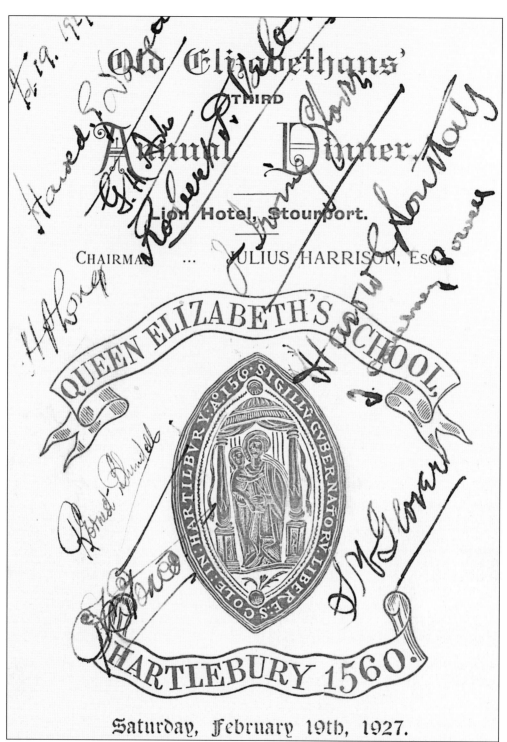

Old Elizabethans' dinner at the Lion Hotel, 1927. One of the courses was Severn salmon. The signatures record a gathering of leading figures of the time. One of them is J. Irving Glover, organist of Wilden church, with whom Julius Harrison had studied several instruments.

Ten
From the Family Album

The following chapter gives a few examples of the often unique record that is saved for posterity in the background of family photographs. This photograph shows cottages in Parkes Passage (once known as Parkes Alley), later the site of bungalows built by the council. On the left are Fred Harris, Eliza and Mrs Rowley.

Eleanor Stokes with her grandson Peter, son Riley and mother Mrs Wall, outside No. 14 Lion Hill (once called Union Row), in 1933. The photograph also happened to record the railings, the elegant sash windows the terrace once had, and the old road level. Next door to the right, now the Bell car park, was the Hunleys' house, which stood forward on the road (see p. 23). There was an upstairs room, once a schoolroom, with an outside staircase. This old house was photographed by Eric de Maré in 1948 (*The Canals of England*) and by Arthur Watts in 1954 (BW Archive).

Jean Jordan with Phyllis Bourne at the back door of No. 11 Lion Hill, 1938-1939. The terrace was extended and modernised in the fifties.

Two snapshots of Sion Gardens in 1935. The grandchildren of Emily and Harry Buckley, boatbuilder, pose with their Silver Jubilee decorations and leave a happy reminder of the sunny row of Georgian cottages off the High Street.

The path by the beautiful garden of Stourbank House in the 1920s. Sitting on the bank is one of the sons of F.D. Ratcliff, manager of the vinegar brewery, who lived at Stourbank House. The path originally ran from Lichfield Street across the fields and along the Stour to the Severn.

The south side of York Street and the basins were in Stourport's first conservation area, given 'outstanding status' in 1975. This aerial view, taken in the late 1950s, shows the eighteenth century wharfingers' houses and walled gardens fronting the basin and wharves.

Acknowledgements

The compiler and Stourport Civic Society would like to thank members and friends for the tremendous help we have received. We hope that still more people will feel encouraged to let us know of old photographs they have so that the record of our town can be copied and preserved.

We owe special thanks to Fred Bevan and to Geoff Neal, who has been closely involved in creating this book; and to Audrey Cooper, Colin Harrison, Philip Worthington, Phil Garrett, Barrie Gould, Jack Knight, Florence Phillips, Raymond Franks, Eva Jones, Margaret Downton, Geoff Bishop, Angela Bishop, Jane Robinson, Eric Danks, Brian Painting, Joyce Rafferty, Jean Horne, Margaret Eades, Rita Phillips, Charles Purcell, Anne Glass, Brian Bird, Roy Baylis, Jean Reeves, Michael Nagington, Annette More, Jack Mills, Jill Fairbrother Millis, the Griffiths family, David Bourne, and to Francesca Llewellyn for writing the introduction.

We acknowledge kind permissions from Wyre Forest District Council, Diocese of Worcester, National Waterways Museum Trust, The Boat Museum at Ellesmere Port, Nestlé UK, *Shuttle Times & News*, British Waterways Archive (p. 22 top), Aerofilms Ltd (p. 25), TP Activity Toys, Pyms Gallery (p. 44 top), Wesley Methodist Church, Worcestershire County Record Office, Worcestershire County Museum, Carpets of Worth, Morgan Advanced Ceramics, Parsons Chain Company, Stourport Boat Club, P.J. Garland; and we are very grateful for loans and assistance from Lady Baldwin, Steve Smith, A. Bone, Mrs D. Weaver, J.W. Bullock, Mrs M. Wadeley, Max Sinclair, John Gittins, K.F. Davies, K.G. Barham, Sylvia Sewter, Mrs D. Baylis, Stanley Barten, W.D. Bickerton, Mrs M. Simms, Mrs F. Humpherson, Brenda Badham, Mrs L. Henfield, Mr and Mrs T. Walker, Melvyn Thompson, Mrs Jones of Netherton, Lesley Potter, Mrs A. Garfield, Jim Perry, J. Hodges, R. Stokes, Miss N. Gill, W. Millward, M. Brookes, R. Jones, G.W.B. Jackson, Helen Caldwell, John Harper, J.P. Thomson, Gordon Thomas, Mary Southall, Daphne Moone, Mrs O. Waddon, Carol Fullelove, Roy Crowe, Horace Haywood, J. Wheeler, Muriel Smith, M-R Benton, and many others.